Days Bright With Laughter

Peggy Moffitt Earnest

Photography by

Nikki Keldsen

Peggy Earnest

Peggy Moffitt Earnest

DEDICATION

This book is dedicated to all families of children with special needs, for their endless love, acceptance, innovation and resilience. You are an inspiration to those whose lives you touch.

ACKNOWLEDGMENTS

I would like to gratefully acknowledge the families who participated in this project. Thank you for sharing your time and for allowing us to try to capture the incredible beauty of your children.

I would also like to recognize a very special group of open-hearted and talented young women who helped make this project possible:

Danielle Earnest
Emma Starkel
Kersten Scanlon
Shaleen Barrett

I would like to thank Nikki Keldsen for her help with editing and for sharing her amazing photography talents.

I would like to thank Amy Bashian McCoy for the motivation to create this book.

Finally, I would like to recognize Megan Masterson, who, before she was even born, was the first and true inspiration for the original poem.

May your childhood joys be endless

May your carefree spirit soar

And may each brand-new tomorrow

Bring you bright worlds to explore

May the sun be warm above you

May God be by your side

And when darkness falls upon you

May the angels be your guide

May you be rich with inner beauty

May you speak the words of truth

May your heart hold pure compassion

And the simple faith of youth

May you know the love of family

May you never feel alone

And may you find a warm and peaceful place

In the open arms of home

May your days be bright with laughter

May your every dream come true

And may you somehow know
The joy you've brought

Since God blessed us with you.

Thank you for supporting Days Bright With Laughter

"We all deserve sunshine and laughter."

Made in the USA
Columbia, SC
31 March 2018